THE *featured* **Pianist**

FREE hints and tips downloadable
to your computer.
Visit: www.featuredseries.com
Registration is free and easy.
Your registration code is: MP480

Boston Music Company
part of The Music Sales Group
New York/Los Angeles/Nashville/London/Berlin/Copenhagen/Madrid/Paris/Sydney/Tokyo

Published by
Boston Music Company

Exclusive Distributors:
Music Sales Corporation
257 Park Avenue South, New York, NY 10010 USA

Music Sales Limited
14-15 Berners Street, London W1T 3LJ England

Music Sales Pty. Limited
120 Rothschild Street, Rosebery, Sydney, NSW 2018, Australia

Order No. BMC-11924
ISBN 0-8256-3477-6

Translated & edited by Rebecca Taylor.

Printed in the United States of America by
Vicks Lithograph and Printing Corporation

Your Guarantee of Quality:
As publishers, we strive to produce every book
to the highest commercial standards.

The book has been carefully designed to minimize awkward page turns
and to make playing from it a real pleasure. Particular care has been given
to specifying acid-free, neutral-sized paper made from pulps
which have not been elemental chlorine bleached.

This pulp is from farmed sustainable forests and
was produced with special regard for the environment.

Throughout, the printing and binding have been planned
to ensure a sturdy, attractive publication which should give
years of enjoyment.

If your copy fails to meet our high standards, please inform us
and we will gladly replace it.

www.musicsales.com

Solfeggietto

Music by Carl Philipp Emanuel Bach

Prelude No.1 In C Major

Music by Johann Sebastian Bach

Two-Part Invention No.8 In F Major

Music by Johann Sebastian Bach

Moonlight Sonata, Op.27, No.2

Music by Ludwig van Beethoven

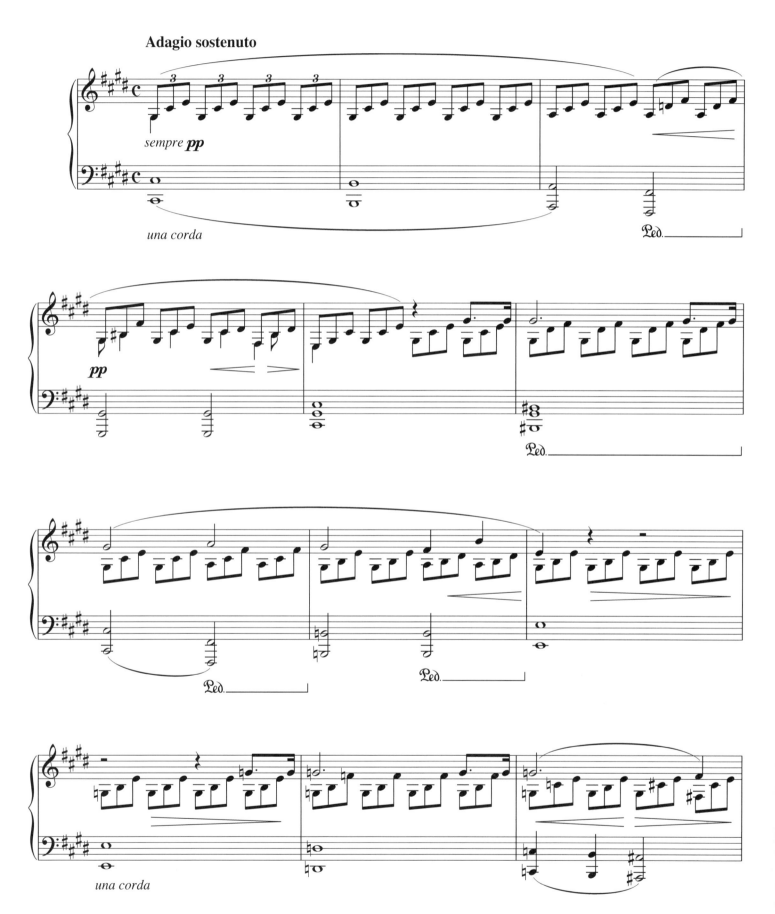

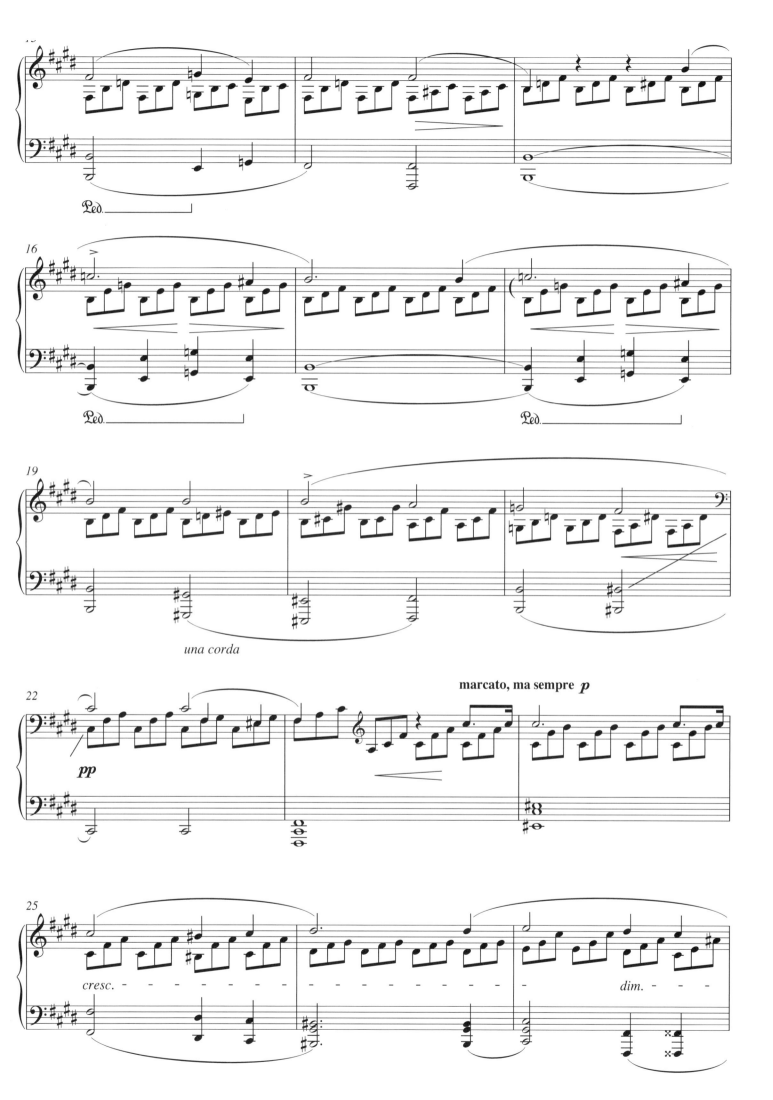

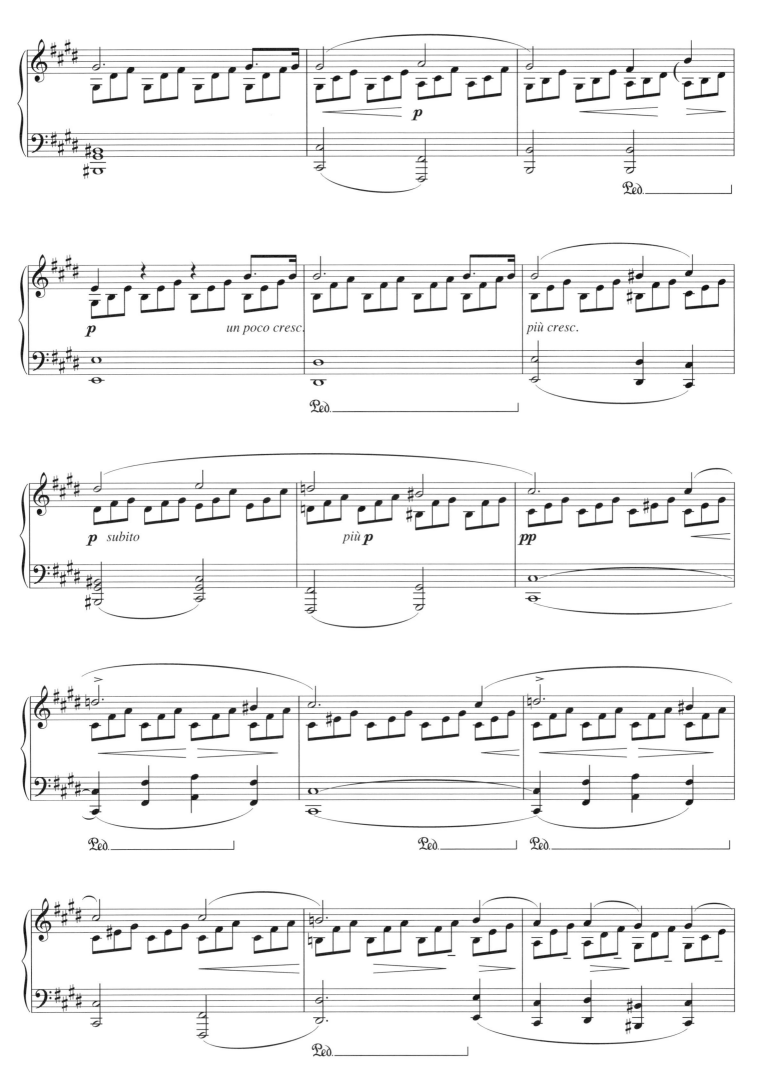

sempre legatissimo

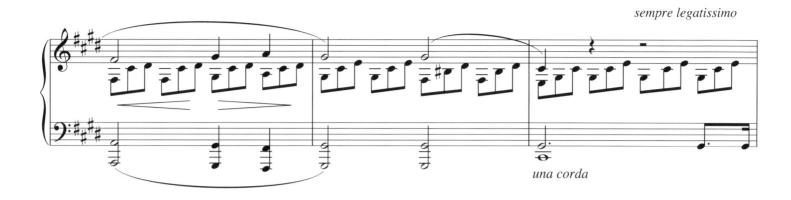

una corda

slentando

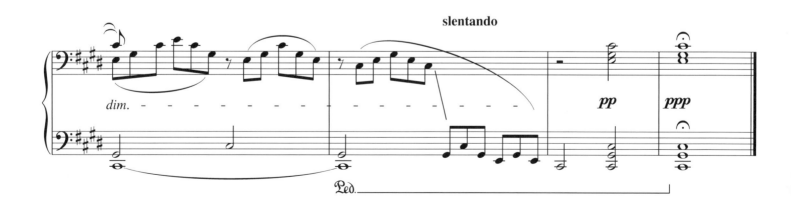

Sonata In C Minor, Op.13, 'Pathétique'
(Second Movement)

Music by Ludwig van Beethoven

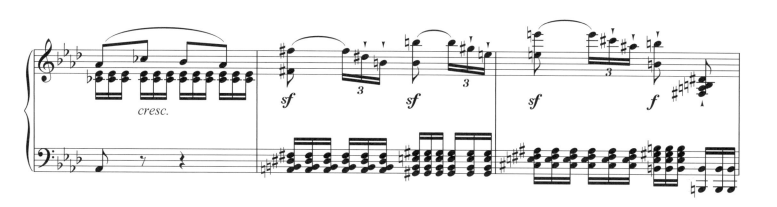

Nocturne In E♭, Op.9, No.2

Music by Frédéric Chopin

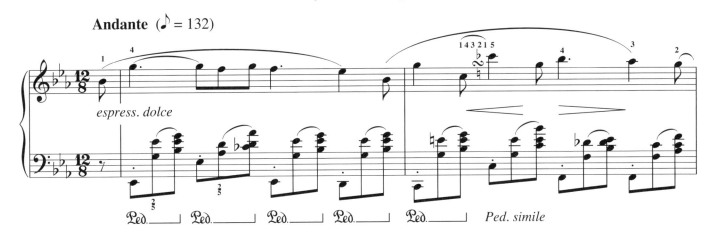

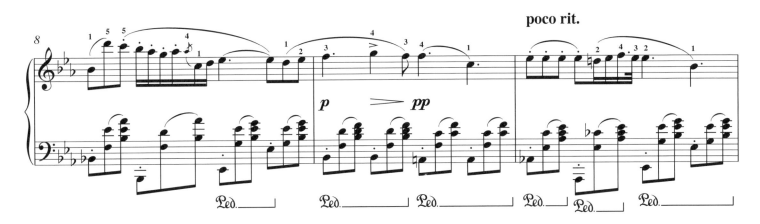

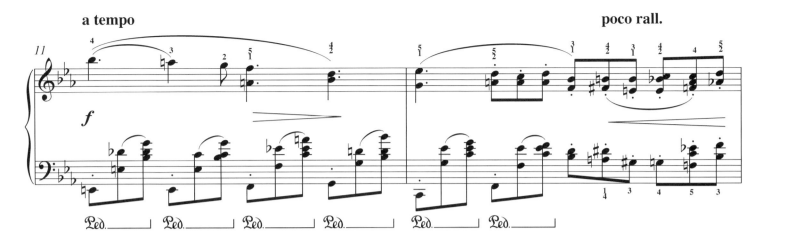

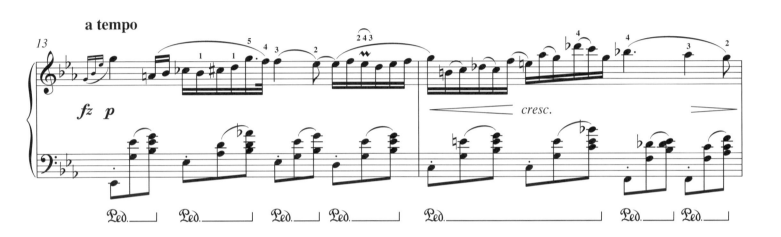

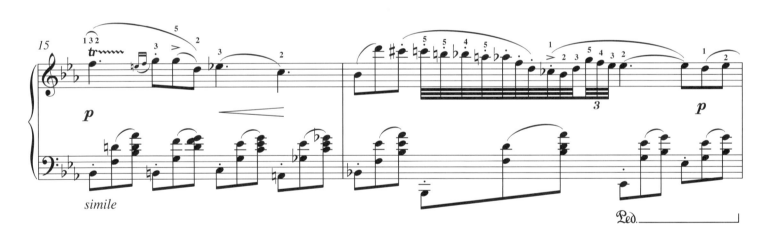

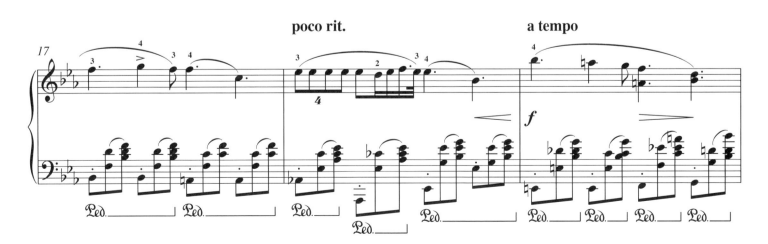

poco rall.   a tempo

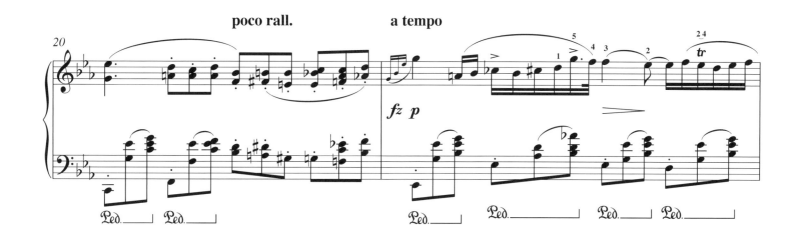

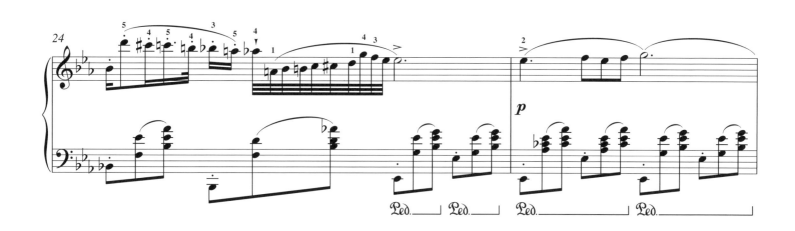

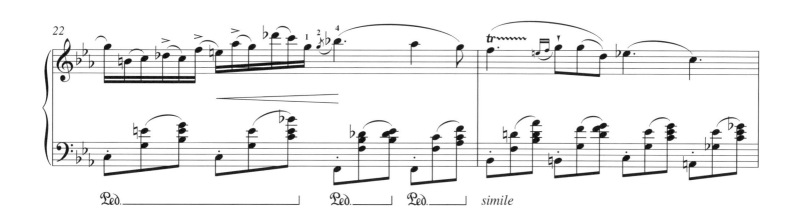

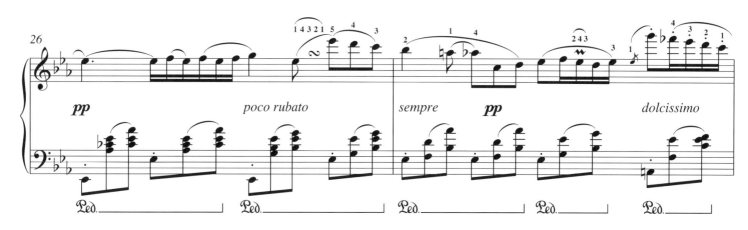

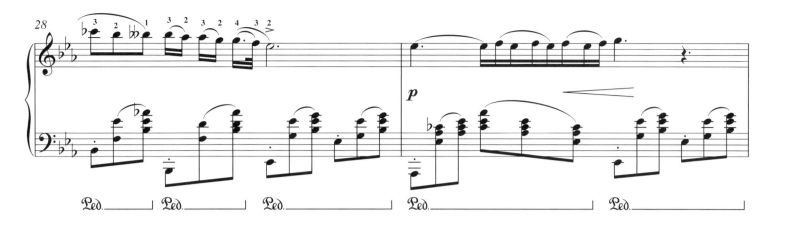

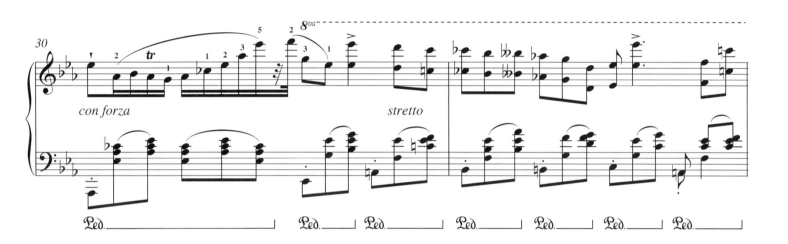

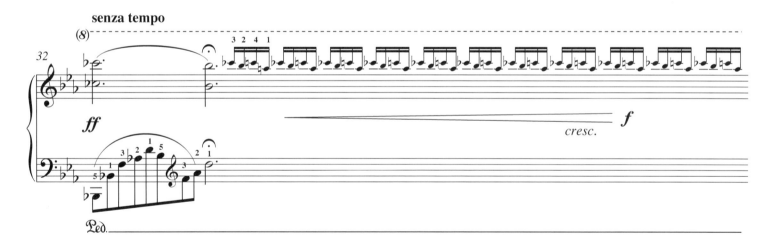

Prelude In D♭ Major, Op.28, No.15, 'Raindrop'

Music by Frédéric Chopin

dim. e rit.

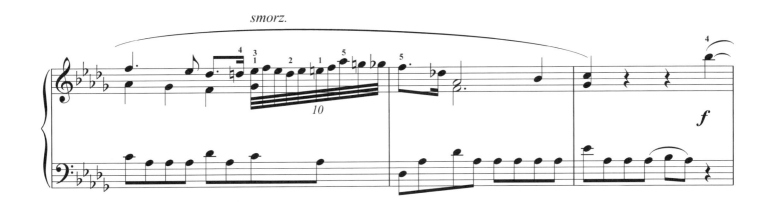

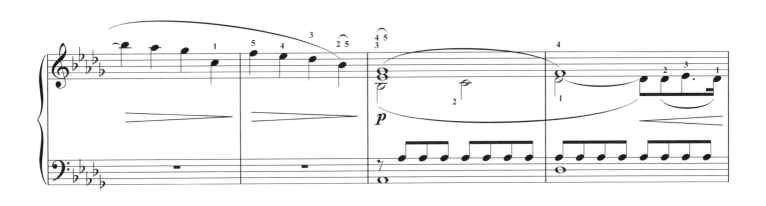

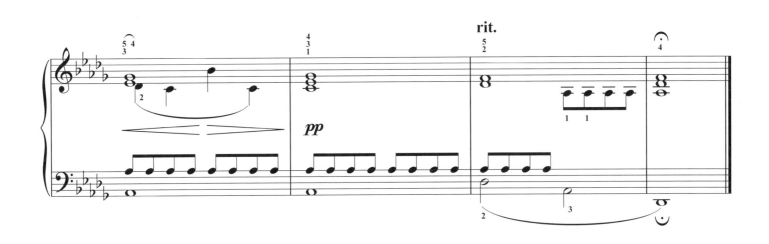

Arabesque No.1

Music by Claude Debussy

Clair De Lune

Music by Claude Debussy

Andante très expressif

peu à peu cresc. et animé

un poco mosso

dim. molto

pp

Calmato

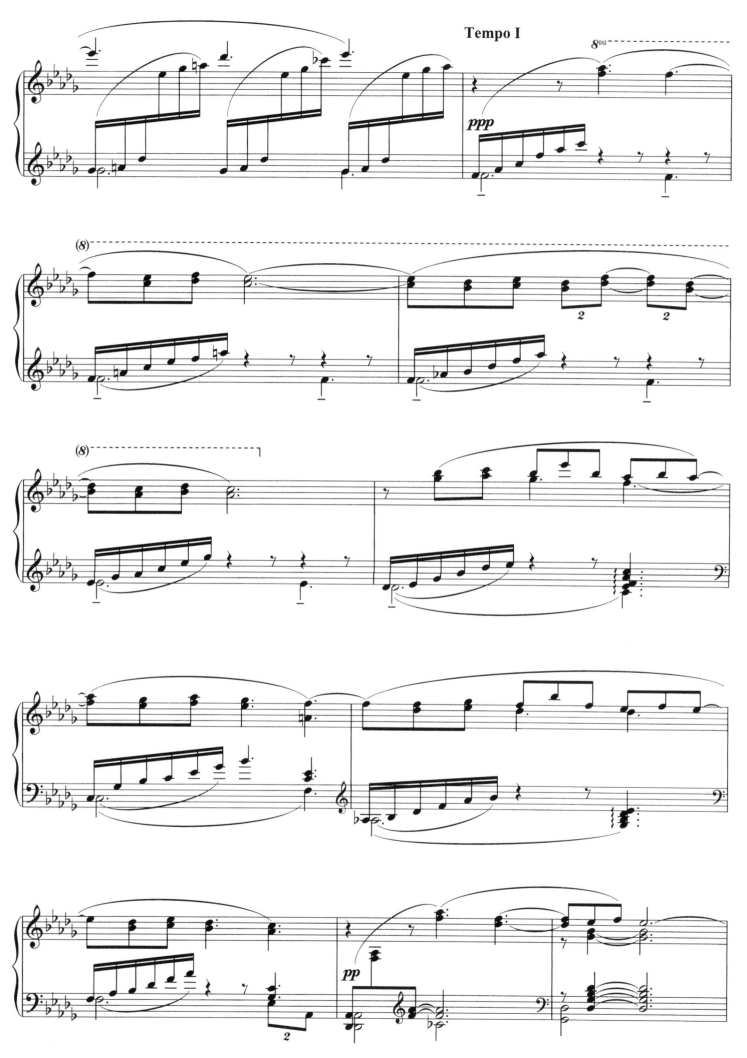

pp morendo jusqu'à la fin

Song Without Words, Op.17, No.3

Music by Gabriel Fauré

41

poco rit.

a tempo

cresc. molto

f

dim.

Après Un Rêve

Music by Gabriel Fauré

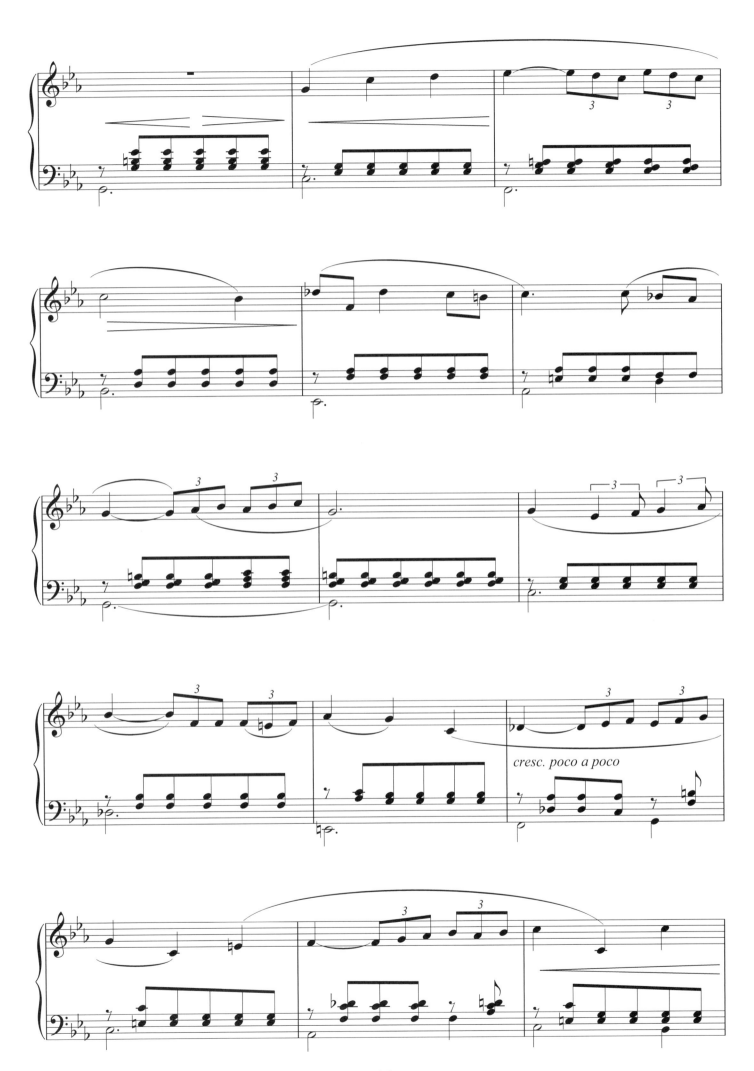

cresc. poco a poco

Sweet Remembrance

Music by Felix Mendelssohn

Impromptu No.3 In G♭ Major

Music by Franz Schubert

51

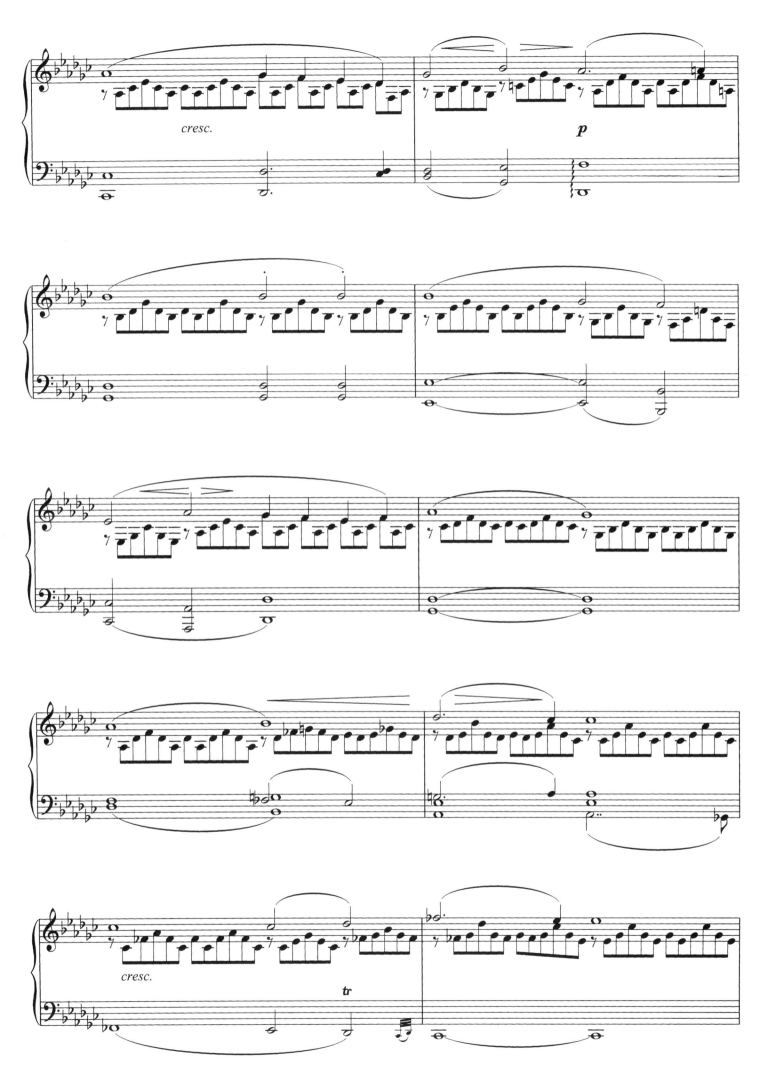

Piano Concerto No.21 In C
(2nd Movement: Andante)

Music by Wolfgang Amadeus Mozart